D1444647

DEAR DELINQUENT

DEAR DELINQUENT

ANN TOWNSEND

SARABANDE BOOKS
Louisville, KY

Copyright © 2019 by Ann Townsend
All rights reserved.

No part of this book may be reproduced without
written permission of the publisher.

Library of Congress Cataloging-in-Publication Data

Names: Townsend, Ann, 1962– author.
Title: Dear delinquent : poems / Ann Townsend.
Description: First edition. | Louisville, KY : Sarabande Books, 2019.
Identifiers: LCCN 2018030467 | ISBN 9781946448347 (print)
Classification: LCC PS3620.O958 A6 2019
DDC 811/.6—dc23
LC record available at https://lccn.loc.gov/2018030467

Cover and interior design by Alban Fischer.
Cover image © ddukang/Adobe Stock
Manufactured in Canada.
This book is printed on acid-free paper.
Sarabande Books is a nonprofit literary organization.

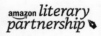

This project is supported in part by the National Endowment for the Arts.
The Kentucky Arts Council, the state arts agency, supports Sarabande Books with
state tax dollars and federal funding from the National Endowment for the Arts.

CONTENTS

DEAR DELINQUENT

HOW EXCESSIVELY I LOVE

How excessively I love, how
trouble carries me from ship to ship.
You've taken me from sorrow
to sorry, yet each time
I walk away I'm unmade
until, dressed or undressed,
only error draws me forward.

Still I want my knight, each night,
in my naked arms, want your face
flushed, by joy transformed,
want you to use me as your pillow.
You transfix me more than Floris did Blancheflor.
My heart, my eyes, my nimble
mind, *bel amics*, fairest friend and foe,

when will you bow to me?
When will we lie again at night
trading clever kisses?
Though I carry another's name,
yours tastes alive against
my tongue. Go on, this letter says:
give me what I want.

(After Beatriz de Dia, "Estat ai en greu cossirier")

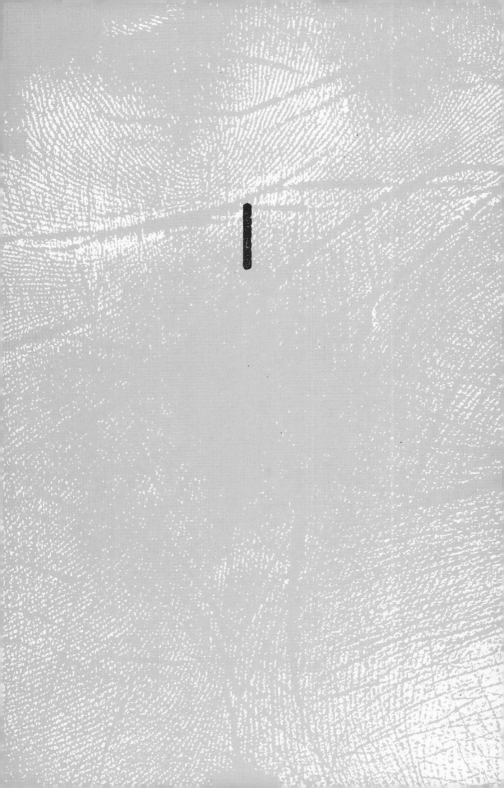

LIFE LINE

We're in for a veritable songfest,
you say, as each child tunes

an instrument into submission.

A hush, then cacophony—
arrayed in rows, all mangle

"Frère Jacques" together, and among

the blats and quacks and enthusiastic
drumbeats, our own lovely piccolo

tugs down her skirt, her eyes

play madly about the audience, mouth
askew. Now is not the time

to take the picture. The teacher

tapping time with a cardboard baton,
the audience unraveling,

and me gritting my teeth,

building my jaw muscles apace,
though this, by itself, isn't news

until you reach for my hand,

and look askance at the life line.
It will be at least exciting, you say, if not long.

LET ME PUT IT LIKE THIS

When he asks for the truth
I tell the part he likes to hear,

how my lines
were drawn   on his template,

stamped and pressed
from that first mold,

so the seam shows sometimes.
He finished

the kitchen counter   and called me to see.
Proud of his fabrication,

he dipped his gaze
to the backsplash, its coved edge

hiding the crease so no grime
would ever gather along the invisible

joint, resulting, he said, in the highest
durability. He stroked the counter,

commending its smoothness, ran a hand
as if across the flank of a cooling horse

and failed to see me stilled
—his fault or mine only the gods could say—

and laid bare against the wall,
its skin painted that morning,

most sanitary, most pristine,
remaining this white   every day forever.

Am I to be known by my wound?
was the thought that kept circling,

that picked idly at me, visible edge
fraying, though no blood, as yet.

WHY HE DIDN'T SAY IT

He scanned the evidence
    she left behind, the soiled, modest display

of her dressing table, lip pencils
    and other crumbs of beauty mingling

with the morning's optimism before
    speech started in with its erosion.

She was like, he thought, a name in a book,
    fixed in print, opaque. A puff

of powder lingered, or the veneer
    of perfume sprayed perhaps the day before.

Latticework of dawn across the table,
    wool rug thinning beneath his feet—

he counted on these facts as on the fingers of a hand.
    Then sound returned as a whine in the pipes,

a door opened, and rattling into the room
    came her agitation. The shutter flung out

its aperture. His eyes blinked.

> The door closed behind her,

and so the familiar insomnia

> of marriage descended again.

THE SEAL

Because you've gone to seek your fame
        on another stage, and because
my legs grow strong on rage and running
        and summer peaches ripen
insistently, reminding me
        of your mouth on mine

when I was ten, because the fruit in jars
        is flecked like the skin of your hands,
because I twist the lids to seal them
        and leave them cooling
on the counter, because
        I run away each time but then

come back, and in running defy
        my hunger, each morning I test
the seam with the blade's
        careless edge. Each morning
—how many days?—
        I unlock the lid from the jar.

THE LATE ASH TREES

Needles rained in the pine grove.
   Acorns tumbled in the tall grass.

I was about to inflict phenomenology
   upon the oak trees. I was about

to dispense some prescription
   like a film of dust to coat the leaves,

with chainsaw at hand, my remedy
   a razor's edge. Then the wind

that held and released the trees
   spread before me its haze of pollen.

Behind me, butterflies self-immolating
   on the compost heap.

How softly they speak. The hawk
   that settled on the dying ash

curled his claws in inquiry
   around a limb pocked

with D-shaped excisions,
      what the emerald borer had

consumed and left behind. How swiftly
      they go, from each and all.

RACING SEASON

What's it called when they stitch
the thoroughbred mares so

they can't breed? he asked.
The Caslick procedure, she said,

nodding to the mare in the next pasture
who'd jumped the fence to mate

anyway, pulse thrumming through
the lumen, something empty

in her to fill. Torn, yet
calmly she clipped the grass

with her square teeth. Horses
only know the present tense,

she said. They're made that way.
The mare's monocular eyes

flicked up, watching. Unbridled
and by default alert in the field.

Now testing with her teeth
the fence's one rotten board.

EARTHWARD

The shovels sing their song
of hitch and heft as we walk the rows

pulling potatoes and beets from the earth.
Needled, bright, the sun's resinous light

flickers behind my eyes like dark matter
on a radar screen. As you bend

for what you've unearthed—
Solanum tuberosum, of the deadly

nightshade family, which is to say
the common potato in its jacket of dirt—

your curls graze your face, the sweat
that bleeds there. You brush them back

and leave behind a mark, a calligraph
of dust that wavers its signature

across the bridge of your nose.
It's then, as the sun steps between us,

that I see your younger sister trailing you.
Her faceless face, that I never met

except in dreams, that even now
drains away, leans to tell of the compact

we made, and of her disappearance.
Then the sprinklers oscillate

and spit the water rich with iron
and we run but she does not.

From a distance, as the wind rolls
across the canvas and the gladiolas

wave their goodbyes, someone might
mistake the water, as it plays across

her body, for breathing. Someone might
call after her, *come inside.*

HERE BE DRAGONS

A compound smell of ink and roses
in that room kept unflowering

     though the candle went unburned,

tightly wrapped in its red cathedral
of wax. Irony floated around

     pollinating the ordinary words.

From sunlight through slatted blinds
motes of dust sifting and rising,

     as if the room's past lives,

rented lives, checked in and out,
had left behind an efflorescence—

     how they were enchanted, how erased—

so body from body sadly divided
we left our own haze of pity

     and pleasure behind until one day

it was rendered like this: that first
you knew me for my words alone,

and now I sing of all I'd rather not.

LIVES OF THE TROUBADOUR POETS

after Arnaut Daniel, Chansonnier N,
Pierpont Morgan Library Collection

I am Arnaut, who weeping
and singing go—
ink-flecked, on horseback, tucked
in a messenger's pack, its corners

rubbed and softened, his canso
came flying. *I am Arnaut, who gathers*
up the wind. No matter
he'll never sing again,

what he said lives beyond
designation, beyond law,
bound and catalogued
in the Morgan Library, parsed out

in an uncial script so cramped
and impossible I have to trust
the transcriptionist after all.
I touch it with fingers gloved

in cotton. For five years,
thousands of pages have passed

between us. Now your email
blinks at me, unopened:

How, my darling, will you praise me today?

MERETRICIOUS KISSES

I eased the straps from my shoulders
and let them drop. Cupped and tensed
my palms, satin aslide beneath
my fingers. Soft my breasts,
but I was cool, waiting, uninvolved.
Him in the chair, legs asprawl.

The mind knows when to stand back,
let the dance have its say. Reached
behind me, thumb and index finger
deftly unhooking. Part of me
was not for order, but chaos.
The Latin word is *hibernaculum*,

winter residence, shell encasing the bud,
and I sheltered us both, at least
for the course of my undressing.
Memorable for him, I thought.
He liked everything I did
and, later, everything I made him do.

ERRORS OF BEAUTY

So much for the sublime, he said,
        pulling on his jeans, left leg, right leg,
               until, fully clothed, he surveyed

love's debris. Despite how many
        years of practice, the present tense insisted
               on residing in the details—

I did it with my body,
        said the pillowcase, mildly embroidered.
               A cup of water could be seen

to quiver occasionally, the surface tension
        broken by a motion not its own. Permanently
               disturbed by passion, the room

rearranged its pieces—all, that is,
        but the one left sprawled on the sheets.
               In its abandon, that body never changed.

THE SPRING OF LIFE

The newts swam agitated in the jar
he cradled in his hands and held
toward three girls on the bank,

while I crouched on the hotel bathroom's
cold tile, bile on my tongue.
What a terrible painting, I thought,

then threw up in the sink.
The newts jostled against the glass
until water dampened and feathered

the lace of his cuff.
From my vantage point on the floor,
the painting felt filled with PRESSURE.

The title, seen from an angle:
The Spring of Life.
His shoes were wet with mud,

spring water quickening at his feet.
These girls, their dresses
pintucked across the bodice—

One looked unhappy.
One looked enraptured.
One looked stupid but perhaps

the bathroom light failed to flatter her.
That day the newt on the ultrasound
was no larger than a peppercorn.

Five weeks along, the sonographer said,
scrolling the wand across my belly
as she scanned what swam inside.

It's so small, I said.
My voice had love in it.
Still at 1:50 I swallowed the pills.

I could throw them up—I could—
was the thought minutes past.
You'll expel the uterine contents

eventually, the doctor said
from far behind her desk.
It took four days,

then into my hand you swam,
faceless face curled in a puddle,
sliding against the placental blood,

the cord a length of thread quivering.
Grapeskin, mucal smear I cradled
in my palm. Look, he said,

at the newts in their jar
swimming briskly in their orbit.
One girl held her skirts in fists.

One girl reached for them.
Look, he said. The water swirled
and eddied with the motion

of his wrist. Naked in your blood
you curled, asking your impossible question.
I weighed you in my hand,

slipped you into a soft wrapper,
kissed the wrapper,
tucked you beneath the roots of a tree.

What tree I will not say—
let them look and never find you.
I pressed my foot down

to close your door.
Of course I loved you,
even as I set my heel against the dirt.

EPITAPH FOR TWO

Forward goes the clock,   forward your weeping—
no way to smooth   what's embedded behind

the eyes, scribbled there,   scored as on a wax
tablet, encaustic.   No way to erase

it, recursively burned in.   So forward
you spooned   the admixture of Ambien

and juice into his mouth,   forward you pressed
the blade between   the tendons that shielded

his bluest vein, faint line   drawn from thumb joint
to the elbow's   tender crease, opening

him. Forward the pulse   that knew no other
way. You laid   him there, you joined him there

on the dining room rug.   But last month, he ate
a slice of apple   from my hand. Opened

his mouth for me. You   looked at me, then past
me, toward   what? The hotel waiter, bearing

breakfast? The row of   yellow chandeliers?
Some bitter truth   born aloft like a thread

unwinding in the air?   You looked for it,
leaned toward it,   and his mouth closed round the apple.

HOTEL PHENOMENOLOGY

Each afternoon that week,
another assignation,
all wrong in the abstract

though not in the act.
The hotel room dimmed
and softened. Illicit,

you said, and yet
surprisingly meaningful.
Hours passed.

I closed the door
behind you, pressed
my face against the fish-eye

lens. Time to assume
again your public form,
I thought, and watched

that manifestation
unfold. You stepped
to the hallway mirror

and smoothed your ruffled hair.
With your handkerchief
you wiped your mouth,

braced your shoulders
against the weather,
then turned from the mirror—

which held the only face
you needed to see—
and the elevator took you.

KISSIFICATION

*Basiationes, or kissification, is a word coined by Catullus
to suggest an utterly unreasonable number of kisses.*

I skimmed my thumb against the sleeve of his raincoat
to test how far the current between us

still traveled. His pockets were full of quarters.
Into the meter they fell, and so we parked a while.

On his dash, the hour askew,
so I reset the clock to turn back time.

Do I get a kiss for that, I said.
You can make a poem out of anything, he said,

and motioned toward his zipper. Stroked,
lifted, held in the hand, weighed,

mouthed as the blood pulsed—
he held me, stilled, nape of my neck

tensed against his hand, then pulled me up,
kissed laconically my mouth,

bored or savoring I still can't tell.
Overthinking again, he said, aren't you.

DEAR DELINQUENT

Dear disaster, he said to me,
        tossing my shirt across the room

where the doorknob deftly
        caught it. Inside out, its silk

draped and settled like a caul.
        I was fond of his slippery mind,

could not access it, not completely.
        Having mapped him, blazoned

his parts, sent my ships
        across his sea, having dreamt

the way and its destination,
        I learned how he drew near

to teach me *dear*, how he left
        to teach me *lack*. Still I set out,

quickened by his touch, still I asked,
        Fair friend, what is your secret name?

THE LIGHTHOUSE

Her jawline working—no words spilled out.
They stood at the lighthouse,

beneath the trees there. What
had she meant to say? Her jaw

was a piston, engine of instability,
visible sign on her face.

He removed his eyes
to the water's foam and fleck.

The locked door of the lighthouse
mocked her tiny anger.

Behind it, a staircase fit for a child,
where she might climb and consider

what kind of woman throws herself
to the limestone waves below.

She considered love—
and the staircase, too narrow in its span

to contain her. Love would be better
if she walked through the door at the top.

MILLAY'S HAIR

New York Public Library, Edna St. Vincent Millay archives

Because Norma saved even the grocery lists,
    it was no surprise to find a lock of hair

        coiled and glued loosely into the scrapbook,
crimped and rusty, more weird

and alive than any calling card or photograph,
    letter, erotic or otherwise, sweeter

        than the candy kisses fixed upon the page.
I shouldn't have touched it, but in those days

I was always hungry. Despite the rare books
    librarian lurking, I set my thumb against it.

        Weightless, dusty, it warmed at my touch.
By 1949, all the grocery lists affirmed

the same fixations: Liverwurst, Olives, Cookies, Scotch.
    Liverwurst, Olives, Cookies, Scotch, penciled

        on squares of insipid paper. By 1950,
unsteady on her feet; by year's end, dead at the foot

of the stairs. As I placed the book of relics
                back into its archival box, a single

                        copper wire fell from the page,
        bright tendril on the table. I lifted it,

casket of DNA, protein, lipids, and still titian red.
                Really, was I wrong to swallow it?

THE MIND IS ITS OWN PLACE

Mated and unmated,
starlings swarm the willow
with their devotions

until the tree roils
and sways, wing-beats
sounding the torrent

through which they swim.
Dopamine, paroxetine,
an injection of adrenaline

into the bloodstream
delivers the dissident
fuel I crave for the mind's

pleasure, and for its pain.
Call it one song indispensable
to trouble the branching

arteries. The willow divinates
toward water, switching
in the breeze; it grazes

the edge but cannot
rest there. My fingertips
pressed against my temples:

ten points of sensation,
a vaulted cage where
starlings congregate

to rustle their chaos,
their alphabet blown to bits
in the wind's rush.

Yes, you heard me.
Like an aviary, Plato said,
the mind is full of birds.

A UNIFIED BERLIN

The Junior Minister waved a hand
    toward the courtyard where, he said,

        Goering's private lion used to live.

With him we climbed Parliament's steps,

walls pockmarked still with bullet holes.
    In the conference room the Social Democrats

        passed trays of petits fours and coffee.

We were perhaps insufficient, he said.

His voice, uninflected: They shipped
    my father to Stalingrad. Forty days

    and dead. In the room,

the transcriptionist, the translator,

and security stationed against
    the wall. Some time passed.

In East Germany, he said, at least

it was always terrible. Bad luck, he said,

to be on that side of the wall. Even
the apples were poison. We were

to understand this was a little joke.

He brought the teacup to his mouth,

but did not drink. His fingernails
were tapered and very clean.

When you are the victim, he said,

it doesn't matter who is killing you.

SINCE ALL FLESH IS GRASS

Red leaf, you bring it to me,
        splayed, its own silky handedness
spidered out in yours—

        red as the belly of the fish
you caught this morning
        so late in the season,

all leaves having spun
        into the pond. Certain,
we're so certain

        of our own clement weather,
the grass unbending easily
        from our weight and presence

as we rise. Now only
        the bruise on my foot
reminds me of the tether,

        the hook, the clasp.
And how bored I am
        without pain as proof.

UNBRIDLED

The old bridle hanging from a hook
in the new barn,

its seams frosted with mildew
from the rain,

a line of sweat at the cavesson,
and green alfalfa leavings

in the corners of the bit:
I used to warm it in my hand

those winter afternoons
so her mouth would taste me first.

Now another horse bobs
and ducks against my bridling,

craves a peppermint,
bites the hand,

will not jump the ditch,
and shies away

from the sudden plastic bag
in the field. How sentimentally

the old leather reins hang,
draping no one's neck.

DRESSAGE

Look in the mirror long enough
and you can't hide the involuntary

disclosures your useless flesh
still believes in. Simply to release

the pressure that built up
in conversation with him,

you smacked the cell phone
against your forehead despite

every failure flexing the jawline,
grinding you through your paces,

your parade of learned gestures,
governed, quarantined, convinced,

and trying so hard
to make a virtue of unyielding.

DOLL

On his hand, the ring
I hate. Rest easy,

he writes to her—
nothing happening

here. I wait
in the outer room,

whose shelves
are flushed with

his mother's crazy
dolls. He presses

send, crosses space
between us.

Nothing happening
here, he says,

smiling.
And Nothing

steps forward,
into his arms.

IV

O FELON HEART

What's that music   he said,
alert always to the undertow,

to the tide interrupted.   Who's sick at heart
he said, wanting me to say *no one*,

wanting one body   subject to another
into infinity. What's that wine

you're drinking   he said,
adept at all my mouth wanted to gather.

Why not just say   what happened
I said, aware my words

were retrograde,   and liking
that debased formula, all the power

the tired script of love   still had to offer.
We know that song, its name,

its testament.   We know what rooms
we've stolen through to hear it now.

THE VIEW FROM INSIDE

Like the burr-encased
sycamore seed, she curled
in her cocoon of pharmaceuticals,
steeped in their replacement neurons
like meat in a pickling solution,
like plastique with the wick buried deep—

What do you know about plastique, he said.

Having lived the overdose,
she was not anxious to attempt it again.
Having felt her lover's impatient hand
wield tweezers, pluck glass
from her face—against which he persisted
in breaking things—she wondered

why did he persist, when she never changed?

JEOPARDY

You used to say that sex with me
was just a higher form of curiosity.

You're like my own bad star,
you'd say. Ask me something harder,

I'd say: What's disaster's baseline
etymology? If only we'd been

like the French, you could have kept
your wife and slept

with me. How civilized
to lurk in halls, fuck in haste,

write self-lacerating verse. Catullus
called it *basiationes*, you'd quiz,

so for the Daily Double, I'd say:
What's kissification, okay?

And with that win, because
I'm bright, you'd pinch me

twice, irradiated by the TV's
disastrous, devolving twilight.

FROM HIS CAR

he called me twice, filled the line
with his particular human sound,
engaging, but meaningless
in the details. Hundreds
of vowel-consonant blends
were required to tell what pie
he ate, how the office grew cold
in time with his typing,
how he wished to touch me,
and where.
                    Pull over, I said.
Breath was the conduit
through which his voice
paused, eased, and evaporated.
Sibilants, plosives, his tongue,
his teeth, what he said,
how he said it, lived
outside the laws of logical
systems, except the one
we made that had no name.
And I stood in the stream of it,
letting down the gate I raised
for every voice but his.

PITCH STANDARD

Phone pressed to her ear, pressed
to his voice, blurred, hasty

against the storm spinning
through its vortex. Then a click,

the dial tone's A above middle C,
the dark business of failed

connection. Busy, it said,
being married to someone else.

THE SPACE WE MADE THAT HAD NO NAME

We were naked and together despite
everything: despite your cells dividing
at their source, despite the surgery that
had you pissing blood through a catheter,
despite the tablets you swallowed to make
you hard, the injections when the pills failed,
and, at last, the humiliating pump.
Learning all your body could not do. Which
was when it felt most intimate to me.

We were naked, together, and nothing
grew between us, because, my love, you said
no, no each time you wept in my arms, you
would not touch yourself, or let me touch you,
until gone was that space we made tender
once, tender by our bodies questing there.

A SIGN

He caught breath at the sight of the blood
blister on my palm, flayed, tender,

then set his tongue against it.
Excuse me, that's my stigmata, I said.

All men reach out to know, he said,
testing, probing for pain.

Besides, he said, Theognis knew
a beautiful thing inspires attachment.

But a mouth is a just a hive outwelling
its sweetness, its sting, I said. Beauty dies, I said.

SHALLOW WATER

On the dock with a glass
of scotch at dusk, I spy
the three albino skunks

emerging from the barn
they've elected as their
own. I should have killed them

months ago. Minnows in
the shallows disperse like
the silver mercury

they're bent on becoming.
A dragonfly lights on
my bare foot. I am sorry.

I am not your lotus
flower, no. My hand skims
the water's vinous buzz

and sway until the white
koi brushes against me
her sweet rubbery mouth.

She flicks her tail, lapses
with the waves away when
a bass emerges from

muttering light and cloud,
mineral eye, mouth rimmed
with cartilage raised in

relief, eyes like nothing
that's in the human world.
If I could erase one

thing in this paradise,
it would be you, although
you left me months ago.

V

ALL CLEAR

After the lockdown drill,
the practice playing dead,

      we've come outside

to name the leaves,
come bundled and penciled

      to appease the gods

of civic poetry who torment
little children into verse.

      Today the leaves'

tie-dyed hands spell
the fall around our feet.

      I have to tell them

write it down.
Their cheeks are numb

      with cold and the exertion;

they fill their page with lines,
they need to rhyme.

But one girl shakes her head,

cannot say what she sees,
cannot abide the boys'

raucous rhyming, or the girls

in bunches collaborating
niceness, each one

lining out letters

just like the next,
well-behaved and neatly

dressed. Now as wind

whirls all that's friable
and light, she frees herself

of pen and thought

and flies away, leaving
behind, beneath the leaves,

a pulsing, living thing

that agitates its light
when I touch it—

just a plastic beating heart,

a party favor. Sprinting
back, she gestures *give it*,

then holds it tight,

light throbbing through
a fist whose fingernails

have pressed half-moons

into skin, inscribing there
her fear as the heart

paces out its life in her palm.

THE ABATTOIR

A weanling rabbit, dragged, shaken,
barely conscious or feigning death—
the cats tossed it between them like
a shuttlecock. Well-played, I said,
walking by with my shovel. But
when it ceased cooperating
in its own demise, and began
again, alive, the game took on
a new intensity, and so
I stopped them. The rabbit, one leg
dragging, flattened itself against
the dirt at my approach. I saw
death in its eyes, myself mirrored
back. I could have cut it down then
with the knife in my pocket. But
I knelt, palmed its back, stroked its spine,
felt the warmth and adrenaline
trembling. I lifted it, left leg
dangling—torn, broken, or just bruised—
set it in deep grass. It shivered.
The rabbit and I regarded
each other. It closed one brown eye.
Stilled, so small—the cats would have it,
no doubt, by sunset. I drove
the shovel down against its spine.

ENTROPY ATLAS

I stood on the dock
and rocked my weight

against the timbers.
It wobbled like a chair

whose legs mismatched.
Muskrat somersaulting

in the pond. Silver mist
riffling the water.

See, I said, it moves.
The foreman nodded, said,

It's gotta go, and waved a hand
in that universal gesture,

swept clean. Finally, I thought.
Someone's listening.

LIVES OF THE BRITISH POETS

Loose-limbed, in our typical haze
of limerence and cheap wine, we

fell against the storefront's rain-slick
glass, your teeth against my throat, my

heart's quick anapest between us.
Skidding past, boys on skateboards splashed

water on our feet. Get a room!
one yelled. Inside the bookstore, hunched

behind a bulwark of papers
and maps like the King of the Toads,

the owner frowned and said, Closing
momentarily. So we ran

upstairs where you pushed me against
the British poets, from Larkin

to Owen, Pope to Swinburne. I
could feel Ted Hughes's sharp spine against

mine. Shall I bite your face, I asked.
Bite for the camera, you said,

and gestured toward that convex eye
just then come alive from between

two tattered rows of *Collected
Ogden Nash.* Thus surrounded by

semantics, we resumed kissing
in the room of words matter, in

the house where dead voices sing,
in the land of who gives a damn—

not me.

SWALLOW

One hand trolled for the tree limb,
the other cupped the birdhouse

to call it closer.
The wren shot out—

testament of the senses
winging my jawline.

At the corner of each closed eye,
a web of lines.

Light darted ahead,
swallowing.

You're flushed, he said,
then resumed his kissing.

JUNE BUG

We're on the phone when his wife
arrives home—Shit, he says, having
forgotten her, again, at the station.

I'll finish this call upstairs,
he says to her. But her cadence
from the doorway, toned

like torn fabric, arrests him
and his hand tightens over the receiver
while in Ohio a six-legged armored

insect traverses my desk, lumbers
across the laptop's keyboard,
climbs up the screen's photograph

of us, across our faces, past
the pixilated plane trees, the café table,
sun questing through the branches,

attains the top corner, wobbles,
and falls. It's okay, I'm back: his voice,
at last, its warm enclosure.

No, that's a lie.

There is no photograph.

Not of us. Not together.

THE RED CORSAGE

They wrote her name before they left
in script that wavered in whose hands.

They measured date and height and weight
in pencil on the wall. We know

why they left, know an epitaph
like bird tracks runs across the wall

and ends in blot, in smear, in stain.
Maybe tears. Maybe hieroglyph

of pain or resin red corsage
borne up from what they left behind,

flower blooming from their leaving
when they erased her penciled name.

POST-SURGICAL LEPIDOPTERA

Among landscapes, I prefer the wild ones—
October wind crashing, receding like surf

across a dry sky on this plateau a mile above sea level.

The field yuccas shake, pod-heavy,
and the little bluestem flows permanently south,

bent upon unhooking, grain by grain, its ripeness.

It's how the wind has driven them, seeds winging
through the barbed wire fence into the yucca field,

carpeted itself with bentgrass surging south.

Drifts shimmer against the curb. Inside me
such stillness while the wind scrapes the sky.

Every door has closed, yet the tide arrives each

afternoon, flowing south on its one-way street.
My heart presses my ribcage like a octagon fist

but I am patient as pebbles over which waters

rush toward the jack pine, grass undulating
at its feet, while the single yellow butterfly,

sulfuric star, flies north, north against the wind.

NOTES

"How Excessively I Love" is a translation of the medieval Occitan poem "Estat ai en greu cossirier" by Beatriz de Dia (1140–1175). According to her *vida*, or life story, she was married to Guilhem de Poitiers, Count of Viennois, but was devoted to Raimbaut d'Orange (1146–1173).

"Life Line" is for David Baker.

In "Here Be Dragons," the phrase "that first / you knew me for my words alone" is an adaptation of a line of Edna St. Vincent Millay's sonnet "Sometimes when I am wearied suddenly"; the line "now I sing of all I'd rather not" is an adaptation of a line by Beatriz de Dia, from her poem "A chantar m'er de so qu'ieu non volria."

In "Lives of the Troubadour Poets," the italicized lines are from Dante and Arnaut Daniel.

"Meretricious Kisses" adapts lines from Robert Frost.

"Dear Delinquent" is the salutation occasionally used by Edna St. Vincent Millay in her erotic letters to Salomón de la Selva. The medieval troubadour poets occasionally addressed their poems to their beloved's *senhal*, or secret name.

The title of "The Mind Is Its Own Place" is taken from lines in Milton's *Paradise Lost*: "The mind is its own place, and in it self / Can make a Heav'n of Hell, a Hell of Heav'n."

The title of "O Felon Heart" is taken from the French poet Louise Labé's Sonnet 12: "Ô coeur félon, ô rude cruauté." Labé's line is itself derived from an Old French proverb: 'amour vainc tout fors, que le coeur felon' (Love conquers anything but a felonious heart).

ACKNOWLEDGMENTS

Acknowledgments go to the magazines in which the following poems first appeared, sometimes in earlier versions:

"The Abattoir," *Five Points*

"Dear Delinquent," *Blackbird*

"Doll," *Copper Nickel*

"Earthward," *American Poetry Review*

"Errors of Beauty," *Five Points*

"From His Car," *Connotation Press: An Online Artifact*

"The Late Ash Trees," *Kenyon Review*

"Let Me Put It Like This," *American Poetry Review*

"Life Line," *Tar River Poetry*

"Lives of the British Poets," *Plume*

"Millay's Hair," Academy of American Poets' *Poem-a-Day*

"The Mind Is Its Own Place," *Kenyon Review*

"O Felon Heart," *Blackbird*

"Racing Season," *American Poetry Review*

"The Seal," *Blackbird*

"Since All Flesh Is Grass," *Columbus Monthly Magazine*

"The Space We Made That Had No Name," *Five Points*

"Unbridled," *Connotation Press: An Online Artifact*

"A Unified Berlin," Academy of American Poets' *Poem-a-Day*

"Why He Didn't Say It," *Dragonfire*

Composer Ching-chu Hu arranged "O Felon Heart" for a cappella choir. Its premier performance by the Denison Singers took place on June 23, 2013.

I am grateful for the support provided by the Lannan Foundation, the Virginia Center for the Creative Arts, the Andrew W. Mellon Foundation, and the Bernheim Arboretum. These organizations offered space, time, and support while many of the poems in this collection were written. Denison University provided generous support in the form of a Robert C. Good Faculty Fellowship and a Denison University Research Foundation grant. The sustaining care and patience of readers David Baker, Erin Belieu, Dana Levin, Cate Marvin, and Martijn Steger is everything.

MARTIJN STEGER

ANN TOWNSEND is the author of *Dime Store Erotics* (Silverfish Review Press, 1998) and *The Coronary Garden* (Sarabande Books, 2005). She is an editor, with David Baker, of a collection of essays, *Radiant Lyre: Essays on Lyric Poetry* (Graywolf Press, 2007), and is currently at work on a collection of essays on poetry, translation, and the natural world. Her poetry and essays have appeared in such magazines as *Poetry, Paris Review, The Nation, Kenyon Review*, and many others. The recipient of grants from the National Endowment for the Arts and the Ohio Arts Council, she has also received fellowships from the Bread Loaf Writers' Conference, the MacDowell Colony, the Virginia Center for the Creative Arts, the Bernheim Arboretum, and the Lannan Foundation. She is the cofounder of VIDA: Women in Literary Arts. In 2016 she, along with cofounders Cate Marvin and Erin Belieu, accepted the Barnes & Noble Writers for Writers Award, given in recognition of their work for the larger literary community. A professor of English and Director of Creative Writing at Denison University in Granville, Ohio, Ann Townsend hybridizes modern daylilies at Bittersweet Farm.

SARABANDE BOOKS is a nonprofit literary press located in Louisville, KY. Founded in 1994 to champion poetry, short fiction, and essay, we are committed to creating lasting editions that honor exceptional writing. For more information, please visit sarabandebooks.org.